# The Lobby To Heaven

*The near-death experience of a six-year-old boy*

A REAL-LIFE STORY THAT WILL
LEAVE YOU ASKING MORE QUESTIONS

# *The Lobby*
# *To Heaven*

Written By

John Carr

Platinum Publishing

# Table of Contents

Introduction

Summary

# Introduction

This short story recounts the repressed memory of a near death experience that opened the door to the spiritual and psychic world to a six-year-old boy. Read how the other side reaches out to be heard. Read as neighbors want to be found and continue to reach out day after day after passing away until they are found. Read how others that just have a message to be heard continue to reach out and talk to this young boy through his dreams...

# Chapter One

## Just a Coincidence

There is a young boy who has a dream about his grandfather. In the dream his grandfather and him are sitting on the beds in the room that he shares with his brother. His grandfather would come to their home in the summer to visit. He would sit on his brother's bed and tell him stories about his past adventures. During one of those times that his grandfather visited, he told him all about his life and his travels. His

grandfather was born in 1887 in Illinois. He had
been to South America and back before going on
to fight in the trenches of France in the First
World War. The boy would get to see the scars
that his grandfather got in battle. Always
fascinated with his grandfather's stories of his
exploits, he would be transported to a far-off
place each time his grandfather would tell a
new episode of his life. In this dream of his
grandfather, his grandfather is sitting on the bed
where he always sat during his visits. There
with a big smile on his face, his grandfather
begins to say, "Where I am now is a beautiful
place." The boy looks at his grandfather and
can't help but smile. Then his grandfather says,
"I feel wonderful." When his grandfather says
this a very happy feeling, a feeling of wellbeing

comes over him and the boy smiles back at his grandfather. Then his grandfather continues to say, "You tell everybody, I'll be here when they get here" and wagging his index finger, he says, "You tell your dad I'll be waiting for him."

When the young boy wakes up from the dream. He says, I just had the most amazing dream about my grandfather. He realized that it was very different from other dreams. He didn't really know how to describe the dream or why it seemed so real. He gets up from his bed and he goes out of his room. When he does, he sees his dad walking down the hallway. His dad had a very sad look on his face. The boy says to his father, "What's wrong?" In a low, sad voice his dad says, "we just got a phone call that your grandpa passed away last night". Well, the boy didn't put the two things together. He didn't tell his dad about the dream and he didn't tell his dad what his grandpa had to say. He grows up having all of his friends and relatives come by the same way when they pass away. In a dream, everyone has their own way of sending a message. Now he thinks it's all just a coincidence that all his friends and relatives come by when they pass away. He thinks to himself, "Well I must have just been thinking about them."

# *Chapter Two*

# A Reason to Believe

Year after year go by and the numerous people, friends and relatives continue to visit when they pass away. Those dreams, like the one of his grandfather, stay with him like they happened yesterday. Now some forty years later and he is married with three kids. He takes his wife to a baby shower and there he meets the young mother to be for less than a minute saying, "It's lovely to meet you, I'll be back to get my wife later." Six months later, he's meditating/napping in the afternoon and he gets this young lady that comes to him in the middle of his nap. Just like all his friends and family that come to him in the dreams... right before he wakes up. This is in the middle of the afternoon, so it's not the same as the rest, very different this time. During the dream, the girl is projecting a bedroom and a hallway that they are both standing in and she is looking into the bedroom and staring back at him. He looks at her and looks around trying to figure out where they are and who she is. He doesn't know who she is when she begins to say one thing and one thing only over and over and over. As she continues to look into the room and back at him and she says, "please, please save my baby, save my baby. Oh, please come and save my baby." so compassionately, so filled with emotion. As he wakes up from this dream and he is emotionally devastated. He is very upset and doesn't know why, it takes at least an hour before he composed himself. A couple hours later his wife calls him on the phone. She says, in a low slow voice "Put it on the news, the police and the fire department are at my girlfriend's house her daughter passed away this afternoon of an asthma attack and the baby suffocated in her lap." He says, "You don't mean that girl I met for less than a minute six months ago?" She says, "yes". At that moment a deep somber feeling overtakes him, as he realizes that this is not just a coincidence. It becomes apparent that everybody who has ever passed away and found their way to him in his dreams. Aunts, uncles, friends, strangers and so many more. It has all been for real. He looks back at his life and every year that passes, he recalls all those many dreams of all those people that came by when they passed away. He never thought it was real. Each one plays like a YouTube video so vivid – imprinted on his memory and filled with so much emotion.

# Chapter Three

## Grandma

As he remembers each and every one that had ever passed away. One of the earliest persons to visit is his grandmother on his mom's side. He remembered that she was a very loving person and the widow of a fallen police officer. She raised seven children in the 1930's as a restaurant owner and a cook. He remembers going to South Texas to visit. His mom was raised in the border town of Rio Grande City, Texas. As a family, they would go to visit and stay for a few days always enjoying the time he had there. His grandmother would bake wonderful meringue pies and put them on a shelf in the window for everyone to see and smell. He remembers the first time his family went to see his grandma. She had a porch swing and his mom and grandma sat on it together. He remembers being held by his grandma as she exclaimed how cute he was - just like any grandma would do. When his grandmother passed away, she was the first to come to him through his dream. Until the realization and recall of all the people who had passed, he did not remember her visit. Being so young that he did not remember that she came before his grandfather. In this dream, both were standing in that space, an endless and vast space filled with emptiness. The young boy did not know where they were. He was afraid and had a very uneasy feeling never experiencing a dream so real, it was like being awake in a dream. When she started to ask about the things that he liked to do, it seemed like she was sad. This was not something he remembered about his grandmother. He had never seen his grandma sad or upset so he didn't know what to think. They talked about what he did and how he would spend his time during the day. He told her that he liked running around the backyard and playing with his little white poodle dog was one of his favorite things. This time she was projecting resentful, aggravated feelings as she continued to question him. "What else"? she asked angrily. The young boy told her that he would go to the kitchen and fix a bowl of cereal and watch cartoons in the living room on Saturday mornings. She said, "You can't do that here." She projected a sense of sadness and separation. Now with even more fear and sadness, he wakes up from the dream shaking from fear and he begins to cry. Unsure of what had just happened, he goes into his parent's room whimpering. Standing next to his dad's side of the bed with tears running down his face, he wanted to wake his parents that were facing him... but they were asleep. The boy did not want to wake his dad or mom. He was so confused and could not understand what had just happened. While still shaking from the experience, the young boy knelt down and placed his head on the bed next to his dad trying to get some sense of peace and the chance to calm down. For some reason, he knew that it was more than just a dream. It was so real and filled with so much emotion. It took at least thirty minutes for him to calm down and fall asleep. When he woke up at dawn, he went back to his room and he did not tell anyone about the bad dream. Later that day, his mom was packing to leave with relatives for a trip to South Texas and they told him his grandma had passed away. He was so young that he really did not understand and he did not ask any questions. He knew it was something important because there was such a big frenzy and everyone was sad and concerned.

# *Chapter Four*
## Dream On

Growing up he did not understand how he was able to control different Aspects of his dreams. That is why he did not think much about the dreams when his relatives came to visit. The other dreams were just that, right? When he was sixteen, he had a dream about going to the movies with a new acquaintance. In the dream he and his new friend are standing in the lobby of the theater. When this guy bumps into his friend and begins to pick a fight. This guy says to his friend, "I'm going to kick your ass.". His friend says" no, you are not because my friend knows Taekwondo." The guy says to him, "ok come on, I am going to kick your ass." He steps back and tells the guy "I don't want to fight" and that he doesn't want any problems. The guy begins to come at him, so he slips his shoes off and prepares to defend himself. The guy begins to swing at him, so he begins to bounce on the balls of his feet as the guy approaches closer, he does a roundhouse kick to the side of the guy's head and down he goes. His new friend starts to say" I didn't see the kick. I didn't see the kick". When he wakes up from that dream, he says that dream was strange, however he's not sure why. Asking himself, why is that dream so different from all the others. It stands out from the rest, imprinted on his memory. Going through his day that dream lingers in the back of his mind. He continues to think about the dream for a couple of days. Now as the week progresses, the dream fades into a distant memory. As always, he goes to his brother's apartment to hang out. There he would sit around and play guitar with other musicians. This brother's apartment was where other musicians like to hang out. His brothers were ten years older, so at sixteen, he could hang out with the older crowd. In the following days his brothers invite him over to their apartment to hang out for a while. As they do this, their roommate's brother-in-law Bill comes over and hangs out for a short time. Bill asked him if he would like to go shoot some pool. He says sure and they headed off to the nearest pool hall. When they drive into town, they find the nearest pool hall and go in. The place is full on a Saturday night so after only a short time they leave for another place. When the exit someone bumps into Bill and says "I'm going to kick your ass.". Bill says" no you're not my friend knows Taekwondo." So, the guys says to him ok come on I am going to kick your ass. He steps back and says, "I don't want to fight" and that he does not want any problems. The guy begins to come at him, so he slips his shoes off and prepares to defend himself. The guy begins to swing at him so he begins to bounce on the balls of his feet. As the guy approaches closer, he does a roundhouse kick to the side of his head and down he goes. At that point Bill starts to say the same thing in the dream" I didn't see the kick. I didn't see the kick". Now he remembers the dream and says to Bill "we have got to go". After that dream he thinks that there is something going on but does not understand what is happening or why. He had other dreams but not like that. He saw things in dreams play out in real life but never affecting him directly. He would be aware of being in a dream and controlling different parts in his dream. What he found out later that he was able to do what was called lucid dreaming, A lucid dream is a dream during which the dreamer is aware of being in a dream and can control aspects of the dream, this type of dreaming had been happening for a long time. This time he decides that he doesn't want to know the future. Dreaming stops for a while

and changes in his sleep pattern begins.

# Chapter Five
## Uncle Dutch

Another special family member to visit was his Uncle Dutch, his dad's brother. Uncle Dutch was the young boy's only uncle on his dad's side so he had a special place in their family. He was very nice, friendly and generous. The boy's dad and uncle operated a print shop together as young men before they were married. They were very close and stayed close the whole time the young boy was growing up. Later on, Uncle

Dutch was in the oil business and was a
millionaire several times in his life. He had a big
white house that was very large in the mind of a
young boy. There were many fond memories of
the great times in Houston at Uncle Dutch's
house during summer vacation. Christmas was
always so much fun and his cousins would
receive gifts like go-carts. One was black with
seating for two. He remembers having such a
good time watching everyone taking turns
driving in the big circle drive-way. The night his
Uncle Dutch passed away was when he visited
the boy (now a young man) in his dreams for
the first time.  Uncle Dutch projected the image
of the front yard of the young man's house. It

was like he walked out of his front door on a beautiful spring day. The sun was shining and

there was an unusual glow around the trees. The trees had leaves that were a sparkling brilliant color green and his uncle was standing on the path that lead to the door. Uncle Dutch walked up the path to where he was standing on the porch. He smiled and seemed to be very happy by projecting an intense feeling of joy, a comforting feeling that touched the young man's spirit. He wanted to know where his brother was at. He asked it like he was there to pick up the young man's dad so they could go somewhere. He said "where's your dad?". The young man replied that his dad wasn't there but his mom was there. The young man turned to get his mom thinking that Uncle Dutch would talk to her instead. Uncle Dutch stopped the young man before he could turn to get his mom and he said, "I'll be back for her later." He smiled and there was a compassionate and warmhearted feeling that came from him. The second time his Uncle Dutch visited, was sometime later after he passed away. He came with his first wife by his side. At the time, the boy's dad was having heart surgery and he was so concerned about the outcome. During the visit, his uncle looked at the young man and then at his Aunt Helen and said, "I guess they need another miracle." They both smiled at the young man and he woke up from his dream. The boy who had grown into a young man, was so scared because his dad's surgery was a quadruple bypass and a valve replacement. The doctors were surprised at the surgery. They said that it went faster than usual and that his recovery was remarkable. I believe that was the miracle they were talking about in their visit.

# *Chapter Six*

## Aunt Helen

Uncle Dutch's first wife was named Helen. They all met in college, When mom and dad along with dad's Brother Uncle Dutch went to college in Austin. Just before all of his cousins and his brothers were born. The boy's mom and dad, his Uncle Dutch and Aunt Helen operated the print shop and spent a lot of time together. The boy always remembered seeing pictures of the four of them at the beach and having fun. Pictures of the four of them at his grandma's restaurant. After the print shop, his Aunt and Uncle moved to Houston and his mom and dad moved to Dallas. That's when they bought their first house and started having kids. Aunt Helen was always so nice and happy the whole time she and Uncle Dutch were married. One day the boy found out that his Aunt and Uncle got separated, soon after they separated, the boy and his brothers didn't visit Houston very much. During that time, he didn't see her much and then not at all after that. She was so very nice as he remembers, she was always bringing all the kids drinks and snacks when everyone comes to stay in Houston during summer vacation. Aunt Helen would take all the kids to the movies and then she would take them all to the mall. When his Aunt Helen visited as she passed, she projected a warmly lit space. That warmly lit space was filled with a loving spirit that was extremely optimistic. She projected a friendly cheerful bright smile that made the young boy feel loved and empowered. She was happy and filled with a rejoicing spirit that made the boy feel like it was a comforting warm embrace. There was a message of everlasting love as she gave him a positive and upbeat empowering spirit. She also gave him an acknowledgment of his connection with heaven. He was not sure what she meant or what she was inferring. As she looked at him, she conveyed a warm farewell, expressing good wishes as she parted. Still not convinced that the dreams mean something he continues to think it's all just a coincidence.

# Chapter Seven
## Little Joe

During the seventies, everybody wanted to be in a rock and roll band. Just like everyone else, the young boy had grown up and joined a neighborhood garage band. A brother's band, his two older brothers and the young man formed a band after playing with his high school friends for three years. They were popular in that circle and would play at different people's houses all around town. They met a kid named Little Joe from a friend named Barry that lived on the same street. They would play at Barry's house and Little Joe was always there. He invited the three brothers over to play at his house often because of the big pool house in his backyard. Little Joe was a musician so they had something in common. The three brothers continued to go there for at least a year before they stopped hanging out with Little Joe.

A couple of years later, the young man was napping one afternoon and had a most unusual visitation. Someone he had not seen in some while comes to him in a dream. There is Little Joe off in the distance. The young man is standing in this vast empty space that is dimly lit. It has a solemn feeling coming from within. Then the young man sees Little Joe with an impressive show of agility that seemed to be inexhaustible as he moved around the vast empty space. What seemed like flying to the young man as Little Joe would fly right up to the young man's face and out again. Around and around in a big circle then flying into a figure eight before flying back to his face. He must have done this action two or three times before the young man yelled his name in a frustration. "Little Joe"! He was so upset because he wanted to talk, and Little Joe would not stop flying around and around. Again, he would fly right up to the young man's face and then project a feeling of confusion and bewilderment. Little Joe would fly back to the young man's vicinity and then fly back out projecting hesitation and wonderment at the same time. There were so many emotions and feelings. The unusual place Little Joe found himself in now, with his consciousness freed from his body. This was an unlimited and vast landscape where he could move without restrictions. He struggles to understand what has happened and where he is at. After Little Joe continued this for several minutes, the young man yelled his name again with a feeling of peace and certainty of the place like his grandfather spoke of. As he continued to project a feeling of going into the light. He says with very strong conviction to "go into the light". So off he goes, he flies off to an opening bristling with light and the young man wakes up. The young man never tells someone to go into the light and he does not know why he said that. At the time, he still did not believe that any of this was real. That is the reason for the surprise when he said, what he said, "go into the light" in the dream.

# Chapter Eight

## Bobby

Bobby was one of a dozen neighborhood friends that the young man grew up with. Bobby lived across the street and a few houses down. When they were growing up there were five in the close group. They would play the same street games as every other neighborhood group of kids played. The five closer friends grew up with Bobby who seemed to be the one everyone picked on one way or the other. They saw his older brother picking on him and that led to others doing the same. They went to school together until he left school to get married.

When Bobby passed away, he projected a small white room where they both were standing. He was looking at the young man with a sense of loss and remorse. These feelings, so intense, so real, has a deep impacting emotional effect that stay's with him like the dream. As the boy looked around the room to try and identify where he was. His friend continued to project a feeling of regret as he looked at the young boy. This visit was brief, and the young man did not know what to think of his messages of loss and remorse until later. Sometime later the young man saw Bobby's sister and she told him that Bobby had taken his own life due to the separation from his wife and child.

# Chapter Nine

## Mr. Man at the Gas Station

When the young man was growing up there was a gas station near The restaurant that his mom and dad owned. His dad would take him there sometimes to get air in the tires and get gas. That is when the young man met the gas station man. The young man would go and visit the gas man when he walked around the shopping center. When he got bored at the restaurant, he would go walk around and visit the retailers letting them know that his parents owned the restaurant in the shopping center. At only eight years old, he was very adventurous for his age. He would meet a lot of people during these walks around the restaurant. He made friends in the neighborhood and at the other businesses. The gas man was one of these many friends. He would let the young man watch him work on the cars. When the young man woke from the dream about the gas man, he thought how real the dream was. Just as if he were standing at the gas station, in the bay where they would talk about the day, and the strange thing about the bay was it was white, very clean and unlike the way it was when the young man was there. We stood there, where he just smiled conveying a sense of wellbeing and happiness. The young man was just looking around at the brilliantly lit space. As he turned his head to see outside, he could see into a vast endless white space. He turned to look back and was at the gas station again. As the gas station man is leaving, he says with a smile… then the young man wakes up not being able to finish the dream. There were feelings of happiness and sadness at the same time. Then the confusion sets in and he wonders what it all means.

# *Chapter Ten*

## The Water Feels Great

When he gets back to the age of six he remembers that every year they would go to Houston on summer vacation. His uncle had a huge house and a big swimming pool and they would get to go play every summer in the swimming pool. He looked forward to going to his uncle's house because of the pool. One morning everybody was eating breakfast and he goes out to the swimming pool by himself. He sits on the first step and the water is up to his waist and he thinks to himself that the water feels great. He sits on the next step and the water is up to his chest, and he thinks that it feels even better. He stands up and wades back from the steps and gets further and further away from the shallow end of the pool. Now centered in the deep end of the pool he starts to struggle to stay on top of the water. As the water begins to go over his head, he fights his way back up on top. He is totally out of breath and looks around and does not see anybody, but he does not panic. He really does not know what is about to happen. As the water goes over his head for the second time, again he fights his way back up on top of the water. At this point, he cannot catch his breath and as he looks around, he still does not see anybody. As the water again rises over his head for the third time, everything turns white and a peaceful calm comes over him. Immediately he is floating above the pool looking down, but he does not realize that he has left his body or that he is floating above the pool. He just looks around for a few seconds then he sees the curtains on the sliding glass door start to open. He sees his Uncle Bill standing in the open door and begins to run out to the side of the pool. He takes off his socks and shoes and goes into the water. A few seconds later, he emerges with the young man's body and lays it down next to the sliding glass door. As he does, he says, "I recognize Uncle Bill but who is that he laid down and who is that he pulled out of the water.?" His Uncle Bill gave him a slap with the palm of his hand across the face, a little water comes out and immediately the young boy is back in his body. At that point, he remembers and says to himself "I had a near-death experience. I died, left my body and that is what opened up the door to the spiritual and psychic world."

# *Chapter Eleven*
# Reaching Out

Now with this realization he thinks maybe it is over. He and his wife are moving to a new house. He meets the neighbors infrequently about three or four times in three years that they live there. One morning he wakes up from one of these dreams, he knows is just like all the rest, but this is a little different. This dream is dark and depressing with lots of sadness and sense of separation. There is no image projected but it feels like his mom has passed away. Reluctantly he calls his mom's house and she is just fine. What a relief. Ok, now that it was not his mom, it must have been nothing. The next morning, he wakes up from the exact same dream ...dark and depressing, sadness, separation anxiety and there is no image, but it feels like his mom has passed away. So again, he calls his mom's house, and everything is fine. "Great, it must be me." Night after night, the same dream over and over it continues to happen for 10 days in a row. On the tenth day in the afternoon, he is trying to get in his front door. He has a long path he has to walk to get to his front door. As he takes a few steps walking up the path, something draws him to look across the street. When he does, he looks at the house

that is directly across the street from his house

and he does not think anything about it. He says

to himself "that's Debbie's house - so what?"

and he tries to walk up his path to his front

door. Taking a few steps, again something

draws him to turn around and look at the

neighbor's house. Again, he just acknowledges it

is the neighbor's house, "that is just Debbie's

house" and again he tries to walk up his

path to his front door. As he tries to make his

way up the path for the third time, something

forces him to stop and look at the neighbor's

house across the street. When he does, he makes

a few more observations ... the mailbox is full

and overflowing, previous holiday

decorations are still out, newspapers are piled

up out front. Then all the emotion from the dream starts flooding out of the house at him. He starts to feel all the sadness, separation anxiety and depression. He starts to well up inside and then he begins to tear up. At that point, he realizes "wow" that must be where this dream has been coming from, the neighbor across the street. The neighbor that lives on one side of Debbie is named Kim, an ex-police officer. He calls her, he knows her a little bit better. He calls Kim and says, "Hey, you know Debbie better than I do. Why don't you give her a call and see how she's doing?" Kim calls back and says, "there is no answer." He says, "Why don't you call the police and fire department lets make a welfare check?" She says, "Well, why do you want to do that?" He says, "I haven't seen her in a while, I think its important we should call. I will tell you more later, but I just think it's a good idea that you call." She calls the police. The police and fire department show up a few minutes later. Everyone mills around while the police knock on the windows and doors. After about an hour later they kicked the door in, and sure enough Debbie had passed away back in her bedroom for about 10 days. He waited till everyone was gone before he started to think about telling Kim about his secret. The secret that he doesn't tell anyone until now. Reluctantly he prepares to tell Kim his secret knowing it would be her first question.

# Chapter Twelve
## Family Attachment

Now Kim asked him, "How did you know that she was dead?" He says, "Well, I have friends and relatives that come to me in dreams when they pass away. I always thought that it was a coincidence, just my imagination. This time I have been having this same dream for the last 10 days and I could not understand who it was or where they were. Until today when I was walking up to my house." Kim says, "My brother passed away off a cruise ship in July. Can you call him?" He says, "No, my name is not John Edwards and that is not how this works. I just can't call Heaven. They have to come to me." Anyway, her brother must have been attached to her because that night he has this dream. In this dream, a young man comes to him and holds up this necklace and says, "I have this necklace for my sister." He says, "Who are you and who is your sister?" He just holds up the necklace and says, "I got this necklace for my sister." The next morning, he goes across the street and says, "I never tell anything about these dreams. But I thought maybe just maybe it has something to do with you." He tells her the dream and three months later, Kim's family sends her, her brother's luggage from the cruise.

She is not sure why they sent the luggage to her but she happy about it. She looks through all the hard luggage, the kind with the little pockets and a mirror. She rips out the interior silk lining thinking that her brother may have hidden it there. No she doesn't find anything, but she is determined that her brother sent her a necklace. She remembers a duffle bag that was sent with the luggage. She takes it and turns it upside down and out drops two t-shirts and the necklace. She calls him back and she tells him about the found necklace and how happy she is about the found necklace says, "I don't know what you have going on, but my brother reached out to you from the other side to tell you about the necklace for me." She says, "Thank you so much". He says, "Do me a favor and take a picture of the necklace and text it to me. So I can look at it and it can remind me that it is not just a coincidence anymore or just my imagination. It will confirm that ever since the age of six, it has all been for real. That what my grandfather said was true, that he felt wonderful and that where he is, is a beautiful place. A place where all of my family and friends will be waiting, and we all be there together one day." She says ok and she does. Sometime later he starts to tell his story to a few close friends. Then he tells it to more and more people who say he should write a book. It takes a while for him to start the book, thinking that nobody would believe his story that heaven is real or that we don't die...

# Summary

Something to remember is you have a reason for being here. Your life has purpose and meaning. This life is a wonderful precious gift. One of Gods gifts is Jesus and he is the way to that place that my grandfather talked about. Who you are will continue, it does not stop here; all of your friends and family are waiting for you there, in a very joyful and beautiful place. I am the six-year-old boy and I have a picture of the necklace to show that it is all for real.